THE RIGHT CARER FOR ME

PLUMBER

KATHLEEN A. KLATTE

ROSEN PUBLISHING

Published in 2024 by The Rosen Publishing Group, Inc.
2544 Clinton Street, Buffalo, NY 14224

Portions of this work were originally authored by Simone Payment and published as *A Career as a Plumber*. All new material in this edition was authored by Kathleen A. Klatte.

Cover Designer: Michael Flynn
Intertior Designer: Rachel Rising
Editor: Kathleen A. Klatte

Cataloging-in-Publication Data
Names: Klatte, Kathleen A.
Title: Plumber / Kathleen A. Klatte.
Description: New York : Rosen Publishing, 2024. | Series: The right career for me | Includes glossary and index.
Identifiers: ISBN 9781499475876 (pbk.) | ISBN 9781499475883 (library bound) | ISBN 9781499475890 (ebook)
Subjects: LCSH: Plumbing--Vocational guidance--Juvenile literature. | Plumbers--Juvenile literature.
Classification: LCC TH6130.K53 2024 | DDC 696'.1023--dc23

Manufactured in the United States of America

CPSIA Compliance Information: Batch #CWRYA24. For further information, contact Rosen Publishing at 1-800-237-9932.

CONTENTS

INTRODUCTION

Plumbers are some of the most valuable professionals in a community. When there's suddenly no water coming out of the faucet—or worse, if there's water someplace it doesn't belong—you want a plumber. And you want one quickly!

Some jobs are dependent on the current state of the economy. If times are tough, people can choose not to eat out or take fancy vacations. They might put off buying new furniture or replacing cabinets or carpeting. However, if there's a problem with the plumbing, it needs to be fixed immediately. If sewage isn't flowing in the right direction, it poses a health hazard. Water leaking can raise the water bill and cause major damage to a building. And of course, people need to bathe, and clothing and dishes need to be washed.

Everyone uses the bathroom several times a day. You probably don't stop to think about how it all works—until it doesn't. Then you call a plumber.

Plumbers will install pipes, sinks, and toilets in these houses. Then they'll connect them to the municipal water and sewer systems.

No matter how tight money is, people will always find a way to hire a plumber for necessary repairs.

Plumbers perform tasks that every household needs. They install and repair household fixtures such as sinks, bathtubs, dishwashers, and washing machines. They also fix leaky or frozen pipes and clogged drains. Sometimes they're called for an emergency repair, such as frozen or burst pipes. In older houses, they might be called to replace older plumbing fixtures or use a device commonly referred to as a snake to clean debris that's accumulated on the inside of pipes.

Plumbers also work on new construction. They install systems of pipes in buildings and connect buildings to sewer or septic systems. Since virtually every building, from small houses to huge hospitals, has pipes, plumbers will always be needed.

Plumbers are also involved in renovating homes. Some people may want to install green plumbing systems to conserve resources and save money. They might want to replace old toilets and appliances with high-efficiency models that use less water. Sometimes homeowners want to replace their tub with a walk-in shower to make things easier as they grow older. This requires some adjustments to the bathroom pipes and drains.

Becoming a plumber can be a good career choice for people who want to have more job security during hard economic times. There is no guarantee that a plumber will keep his or her job when times are tough—even plumbers can be laid off from their jobs. However, there are many other reasons why plumbing is a good career choice in any kind of economy. Even when there isn't a lot of new construction or people can't afford to do major renovations, they still need to take care of routine maintenance and emergency repairs.

Plumbers may also have more work in the coming years as people update their current plumbing systems to make them more "green," or environmentally friendly. Scientists believe that human activity has contributed to climate change, warming our planet and causing changes to Earth's environment. People are trying to change the way they live to be more Earth friendly or more sustainable. This includes things like replacing a lawn watered with sprinklers to plants that require less water or can use a drip irrigation system.

A system like this conserves water by delivering it directly to the roots of plants, instead of spraying it all over the place.

In addition, the price of energy keeps going up. Many people are trying to conserve energy and save natural resources such as water. Plumbers can help with this effort by installing energy-efficient plumbing. For example, plumbers might replace existing bathroom fixtures with low-flow toilets and showerheads. They can also create systems to reuse water from dishwashers, washing machines, and showers. These are called gray water systems. Plumbers can also install tankless water heaters that save energy.

Plumbers can find work anywhere. A career as a plumber can be a good option for people who don't want to be tied down to one location for their work. People who want to move to a new state or country can usually get a job as a plumber, although they may need to learn about plumbing codes specific to their new location.

The ancient Romans constructed aqueducts to bring fresh water into their cities. Some of them still stand today.

Being a plumber is an excellent career choice for someone who enjoys making things or doing physical labor. Plumbing can provide a great sense of accomplishment. Once plumbers are finished with a project, they can take pride in having created something useful.

A HISTORY OF PLUMBING

People consider plumbing and sanitation to be among the hallmarks of modern civilization. However, the concepts are actually very old. Archeological evidence of systems to bring fresh water to communities and remove waste dates back to about 2,600 BCE.

Ancient Mesopotamians used clay pipes in their sewer systems. Ancient Egyptians invented copper pipes. Many ancient civilizations had a form of flushing toilet. This involved pouring water into the toilet to wash the waste down into the sewer system.

The ancient Romans transported fresh water into their cities via aqueducts. They had a sophisticated system of public baths and toilet facilities. Unfortunately, around 200 BCE, they upgraded their water system with lead pipes, contaminating their water supply and creating health problems within the population. In fact, the word plumbing is from the Latin root word for lead.

In North America, there is evidence of a system of irrigation canals dating to about 350 BCE. These are credited to the Hohokam tribe of Native Americans.

What we recognize as modern urban plumbing began to appear around the Renaissance. A forerunner of the modern flush toilet was invented in England in 1596 and the first water main was built in France in 1664.

The city of Boston, Massachusetts, designed the first city-wide water system in 1652. Later, in 1829, the Tremont Hotel in Boston became the first hotel to offer indoor plumbing. (Indoor plumbing wouldn't be installed in the White House until four years later!)

In 1815, Philadelphia, Pennsylvania, designed a municipal water system where paying customers could have water piped directly into their homes. Other residents could get free water from city fire hydrants. Philadelphia also became the first city to replace its system of wooden pipes with cast iron between 1819 and 1858.

The first standardized plumbing code was adopted in the United States in 1928. One of its authors was Herbert Hoover, who would later become the 31st president.

In 1855, the city of Chicago built the first city-wide sewer system. Installing the pipes raised the street level of the city, bringing it out of swampy land that was causing sickness.

CHAPTER ONE

KEEPING THE WATER FLOWING

Plumbing is something people tend to take for granted—right up until it doesn't work. We expect fresh, clean water to flow from the faucet when we turn the handle and waste to vanish when we flush the toilet. Without plumbers, we wouldn't be able to enjoy many of the conveniences of modern living. Want a cold glass of water on a hot day? A plumber hooked up the kitchen faucet and connected your home to the municipal water supply. Ready for a hot bath on a winter night? A plumber installed the water heater that warms the water that will fill the bathtub—not to mention the pipes and faucets that bring the water to the tub.

Plumbers installed the dishwashers in a school cafeteria and the washing machines at the local laundromat. How about the local car wash or the town pool? Any place there's water and pipes, a plumber has been hard at work.

Some plumbers choose to focus on a particular kind of plumbing or pursue related careers. They may choose to become pipe fitters, pipelayers, steamfitters, or sprinkler fitters. These jobs will be discussed in the next chapter.

Your local residential plumber is the person you call for repairs and installations in your home. No matter how small the job seems, it's important to hire a licensed plumber not a "Chuck in a truck" (unlicensed handyman).

FACTS AND FIGURES

According to the U.S. Bureau of Labor Statistics, there are currently about half a million pipe fitters, pipelayers, plumbers, steamfitters, and sprinkler fitters in the United States. About two-thirds of them work for contractors. Plumbers that work for contractors may install plumbing in new homes or buildings, or they might fix or update existing plumbing. Other plumbers work outside of the construction industry. For example, they might work on a natural gas pipeline or for the oil industry. About 10 percent of all plumbers work for themselves, rather than for a company. About 25 percent of plumbers belong to a union. Generally, union employees are paid higher wages than non-union employee.

WHAT IS A UNION?

A union is a group of workers in the same profession that come together to improve their working situation. There are unions for many different trades and professions. Unions employ a technique called collective bargaining to negotiate with management. If a contract or dispute can't be settled cooperatively, the union might threaten a strike. This means that all the workers represented by the union cease work and picket the employer until the dispute is settled.

Sometimes, unions cooperate with one another. You've probably heard about one of the large unions that represents actors calling for a strike in support of the union that represents writers for film and television.

Unions work for the good of the workers they represent. They negotiate better wages and benefits, such as health insurance and retirement plans. Unions also work toward making safety improvements in the industry. They're also responsible for things such as uniform workdays and workweeks.

In North America, many plumbers belong to the United Association of Journeymen and Apprentices of the Plumbing and Pipe Fitting Industry of the United States and Canada. This union, which is also known as the UA, is made up of about 300 smaller local unions. Although plumbers are not usually required to join a union, many find that membership in the UA is beneficial. The UA represents 368,000 professionals in plumbing-related industries.

In general, plumbers make the highest salary of all the jobs in the construction industry. Currently, the median wage for plumbers is about $60,000 per

Labor Day was pioneered by the leaders of early labor unions. They often march in Labor Day parades.

year. Of course, not all plumbers make the same salary. Their pay can vary depending on where they work, the tasks they perform, and their level of expertise. For a list of current plumbing salaries, you can check out the Bureau of Labor Statistics' Occupational Outlook Handbook online at www.bls.gov/oco.

DIFFERENT TYPES OF PLUMBING JOBS

Many plumbers work on new construction projects. After all, any building people use needs running water for bathrooms, kitchens, and other functions. Some work on houses. Others work on larger residential structures such as apartment high-rises, or college dorms.

Plumbers also work on commercial structures, such as baseball stadiums, shopping malls, or restaurants. Commercial structures are very complex, since they include multiple bathrooms, fire sprinkler systems, kitchen facilities for restaurants, and janitors' closets. Each kind of new building requires its own specific plumbing system. Some kinds of buildings, such as fire stations, scientific laboratories, and hospitals, have special plumbing needs.

Plumbers install fixtures such as bathtubs, showers, and toilets. Fixtures are devices that are attached to a wall or floor. Plumbing fixtures use water and usually have a pipe bringing water in and a drain to let water out. Plumbers also install appliances that use water but are not necessarily attached to the wall or floor, such as dishwashers, hot water heaters, garbage disposals, and washing machines.

In addition to putting in fixtures and appliances, plumbers install gas lines for stoves and

Frozen pipes need to be thawed very carefully or they can burst, causing serious damage to your home.

heating systems. They install all the pipes that bring the water to kitchen and bath fixtures, as well as the pipes that take water away from them to sewer lines or septic tanks. They also install the connections for garden hoses and lawn sprinklers.

Plumbers fix and maintain the pipes and fixtures they install. They may also work on remodeling projects in kitchens or bathrooms. Or they might update the plumbing in an existing home to accommodate the homeowner's needs. For instance, if a couple decides that they want to heat their home with natural gas, they will hire a plumber to run a new gas line into the home. Often, people update their plumbing because the pipes are getting old, or they want to install more efficient fixtures and appliances.

A plumber may specialize in a particular type of work. However, most plumbers know how to do many types of jobs. Maintaining a solid knowledge and skill base ensures they can always find work.

WORKING AS A PLUMBER

Plumbers work a variety of schedules, depending on the type of work they do. Those involved in construction generally work Monday through Friday from about 7 a.m. to 3 p.m. Those who do residential work such as installations and renovations might work closer to a 9 a.m. to 5 p.m. schedule. However, some plumbers work for 24-hour repair services. These plumbers are "on call." This means they must be available nights, weekends, or holidays to fix an emergency, such as a burst pipe.

PLUMBER'S ASSISTANTS

A plumber's assistant or plumber's helper works under the supervision of a master plumber. They gain experience by assisting in whatever task the master plumber is performing. Assistants do a lot of the grunt work—loading and unloading the truck, fetching and carrying, cleanup, and prep work.

Plumber's assistants need to pass an exam and be licensed in many states. Roto-Rooter, a national plumbing service chain, offers on-the-job training and assistance for workers to continue their education and obtain their license.

In the past, large buildings, hotels, power plants, and manufacturing plants often had full-time plumbers on staff. Now it's more common for such places to rely on outside companies for their plumbing needs. Therefore, more plumbers today work for 24-hour repair services than in the past.

A plumber's workload is usually steady, although he or she may be busier at certain times of the year than others. New construction generally occurs in the spring through fall in most parts of the country, so there is usually more work available for plumbers during this time. Plumbers may work on indoor remodeling projects during the winter and might also be called upon to perform repair work on heating systems or to mend burst pipes. The aftermath of a severe winter storm might include frozen pipes. Some plumbing companies also perform water removal and flood cleanup services.

Sometimes a plumber will work on a big, temporary project. For example, a plumber might work on the construction of a new hospital. When the project is done, the plumber might be out of work until their next project starts. Most of the time, however, successful plumbers go right from one project to the next.

Being a plumber can be a dirty job. When working indoors, plumbers often must work in small, cramped spaces. Fixing a sink often involves laying on the floor with their head and shoulders inside a cabinet. Water heaters and water cut-off valves are usually in basements where mold might be a factor. Sometimes plumbers need to open up a wall to get to a pipe, which can expose them to dust from insulation materials.

Habitat for Humanity is an organization that provides safe, low-cost housing to families in need. They welcome the efforts of both unskilled volunteers and licensed professionals.

Outdoors, plumbers must often work in difficult weather conditions. They must be careful and alert at construction sites. To avoid injury, plumbers need to be aware of the danger posed by sharp saws and heavy pipes. They must also be careful to avoid getting burned while using welding torches or working on steam pipes, and to avoid falls when working on ladders or scaffolding. They need to be aware of their surroundings at all times, use proper personal protective equipment (PPE), and keep their tools and materials neat and orderly so no one trips.

FUN FACTS ABOUT TOILETS

Did you know?

- The concept of a flushing toilet has existed for thousands of years, but many early iterations involved pouring water from a bucket to move the waste into the sewer system.
- One of the first urban flushing toilets was installed in Richmond Palace for Queen Elizabeth I in 1596.
- In the 18th century, Alexander Cumming and Joseph Bramah both patented improvements to the flush toilet.
- Toilet paper was first marketed in 1857 and perforated toilet paper was marketed in 1871.
- The ceramic flushing toilet was invented in 1870.
- Thomas Crapper did not invent the flush toilet. Instead, he improved the existing design into what we now recognize as the modern flushing toilet.
- Sink plungers and toilet plungers aren't the same. Toilet plungers are longer and narrower on the bottom to fit in a toilet drain. Sink plungers are flat.

Some of today's new water-efficient toilets don't even have a tank.

CHAPTER TWO

SIMILAR JOBS

Some plumbers choose to pursue a related career such as pipe fitter, pipelayer, steamfitter, or sprinkler fitter. These four specialties have qualifications and career paths that are similar to general plumbing. Pipe fitters and pipelayers often work closely with plumbers. Steamfitters and sprinkler fitters generally work on construction projects. Another related field involves installing solar-powered water heating systems.

PIPE FITTERS

A pipe fitter's job is similar in some ways to a plumber's. They both work with pipes in buildings. However, pipe fitters install full systems of pipes in buildings. Sometimes they design these systems. They have to know how to read blueprints and collaborate with other members of the design and construction team.

Pipe fitters may install pipes that are part of a building's heating system. Or they might work on pipe systems that are part of a plant that manufactures chemicals, drugs, or other products. Pipe fitters also set up the controls that monitor pipe systems. These control systems can start or stop the flow of liquids or steam through the pipes and can turn on the timers and other mechanisms that start or stop the flow of fluids or gas automatically.

Like some plumbers, pipe fitters may work full time in one building. In general, however, pipe fitters are employed by companies that build or maintain pipe systems. In this capacity, pipe fitters might need to travel as part of their job. Pipe fitters might also work for a town or city water department. Because they often work on multistory buildings that are still under construction, pipe fitters must not be afraid of heights.

Plumbers work only with systems that carry water. Pipe fitters work with systems that carry different kinds of fluids. They need to know how different pipe materials react to different chemicals. Some pipe fitters specialize in using one type of pipe material or one type of pipe system. For example, a pipe fitter might specialize in working with pipes that carry chemicals. Others work on all kinds of pipes and pipe systems.

Pipe fitters handle many different types of pipes. They must know how to cut and weld them.

PIPELAYERS

Pipelayers prepare the area where pipes will go. They dig trenches for pipes using a shovel, backhoe, or other digging equipment. Once the trench is dug, pipelayers position the pipe in the trench. When the pipe is in position, the pipelayer attaches the pieces of pipe together. Depending on the pipe material, they may use cement or glue, or even weld it together.

Pipelayers work outside. Sometimes they work in remote areas or under difficult weather conditions. Like pipe fitters, they might work for a company that builds or maintains pipe systems in various locations. Other pipelayers might work for an employer in one location. For example, they might work for a municipal public works department or a utility company. They could be called upon to lay pipes for a municipal water system, or for other public utilities.

THE TRANS-ALASKA PIPELINE SYSTEM

At the time of its completion in 1977, the Trans-Alaska Pipeline System (TAPS) was the largest privately funded construction project in the world. TAPS cost $8 billion and employed 70,000 workers from 1974 to 1977.

The pipelayers who worked on TAPS had to lay 800 miles (1,287 km) of pipes from Prudhoe Bay to Valdez, Alaska. TAPS is one of the longest pipelines in the world. It's designed in a zigzag pattern that can flex in the event of an earthquake. Sections of the pipeline are raised above ground so heat doesn't damage the permafrost. It's considered an engineering marvel.

The pipeline is monitored constantly and has a sophisticated leak detection system. The flow of oil can be shut down in four minutes.

Preparing the site for these huge pipes probably required the use of backhoes and steam shovels.

STEAMFITTERS

A steamfitter's job is similar to a pipe fitter's. Steamfitters design and install pipe systems just as pipe fitters do. The difference is that the pipes that steamfitters install are used to move water or gas that's under pressure. For that reason, steamfitters need additional training to know how to handle hot liquids and gases. Steamfitters must be certified to do this type of work as well.

Like pipe fitters, steamfitters sometimes work on tall buildings that are under construction. They need to understand how their system will interact with others being installed in the same building. Like pipe fitters, the need to know how to read blueprints, and how to cut, solder, and weld pipes. They also need to be careful of burns and scalds from the pipes they work with. Steamfitters usually work for companies that install steam pipe systems in many different buildings, rather than working for an employer in a single building. They may also be on call to fix emergencies on nights or weekends.

SPRINKLER FITTERS

Sprinkler fitters install fire protection systems and fix existing systems. Fire protection systems include sprinklers, pipes, and hoses. Some systems use water to put out fires, while others use chemical fire retardants such as foam. This is precision work that requires a five-year apprenticeship.

Sprinkler systems are usually not installed in houses or small apartment buildings. Instead, they are installed in public buildings such as offices, schools, high-rise apartment buildings, restaurants, or manufacturing plants. Fire protection systems save lives and protect property. As a result, some states and cities are considering requiring sprinkler systems in additional types of buildings, including residential buildings. Sprinkler fitters may have a secure job outlook.

SOLAR HOT WATER INSTALLER

One of the trends in "green construction" is solar power. Solar power is a clean, renewable, cost-effective resource. It appeals to people who are conscious of the effects of climate change and wish to live more Earth-friendly lives.

There are different types of solar hot water systems available. Part of the installer's job is to help homeowners decide which is right for them. Some systems are better in certain climates. Other factors may have to do with local building codes. This is an exciting new specialty.

Richard Trethewey has been in the plumbing business his whole life. He learned from his father and worked in the family business for many years.

RICHARD TRETHEWEY AND *THIS OLD HOUSE*

Long before "reality TV" and "DIY" were familiar catch phrases, there was a PBS home improvement show called *This Old House*. Richard Trethewey, a Massachusetts native, has been the franchise's onscreen plumbing and heating expert since 1980. He's the founder and owner of RST Thermal. The company connects homeowners with contractors specializing in energy-efficient heating and cooling systems.

CHAPTER THREE

TRAINING AND EDUCATION

Becoming a plumber requires a solid education. Most programs require a high school diploma or General Educational Development (GED). Students who already know they would like to become a plumber should discuss their options with their guidance counselor. After high school, they can go straight to work as an apprentice plumber. Or they can go to college or attend a trade school before becoming an apprentice plumber. Some people work in another career before deciding to become a plumber. For instance, they might work for several years as a pipe fitter before deciding to become a plumber. Some people become plumbers after spending time in a completely unrelated career as well.

It's never too soon for junior high and high school students to begin preparing themselves for a career in plumbing. Professional plumbers need to have good math skills to do their job. Taking math classes, especially algebra and geometry, is an especially good way to prepare for this career. Because plumbers often work with a variety of materials, science classes such as physics and chemistry are also useful. For example, if a client has used a drain cleaner they bought from a store, the plumber needs to know what's in it before they add anything else. Pipe fitters and steamfitters must know what's going to be flowing through a pipe system so they can decide on the appropriate kind of pipes to use.

If your school offers classes in drafting or mechanical drawing, those are also useful. Technical education classes can teach students how to properly use a variety of tools, as well as the fundamentals of skills such as welding. If a language other than English is common in your area, you should consider taking classes. People are always more comfortable when they can communicate clearly.

If you think you'd like to own your own business someday, you should consider any business classes that are available. Regardless of whether you work independently, or open a shop with a staff, you'll need to know at least the fundamentals of billing, payroll, and supplies.

Plumbers rely heavily on math and science. You can get a jump on your career training by taking any advanced classes your school offers.

TRADE, TECHNICAL, AND VOCATIONAL SCHOOLS

Students who are interested in pursuing a career in plumbing may choose to go to a trade, technical, or vocational school. Some of these schools accept students as young as 16 and offer students many of the same kinds of classes they would take in high school, such as English or history. Trade schools provide students with the skills and training needed for a particular career, such as car repair, carpentry, and plumbing. Students interested in attending a vocational school should talk to their school guidance counselor for more information. If there is a vocational school nearby, students can also arrange a visit to learn more.

COMMUNITY COLLEGE OR TECHNICAL SCHOOL?

After graduating from vocational school or high school, people who want to become plumbers can attend community college or a technical school. Technical schools are similar to vocational schools. They also teach skills that will help prepare a student for a future career, including customer service. Technical school programs are usually two years long. Some community colleges offer skill-specific classes as well. At most community colleges, you can get an associate's degree after two years or a bachelor's degree after four years. A college degree can be particularly useful if you plan to go into business for yourself or take over a family business someday.

At community college or technical school, students can learn how to read plumbing blueprints. They will also begin learning about specific plumbing codes. In addition, students will learn special skills, such as welding. Perhaps most importantly, students can take safety classes so they know how to stay safe on the job.

This student is learning to cut pipe. She's wearing safety glasses to protect her eyes and noise-cancelling earmuffs to protect her hearing.

WHAT'S RIGHT FOR YOU?

After graduating from high school or vocational school, students interested in becoming plumbers have a decision to make. They can continue their education, or they can go straight to work. Although recommended, attending a vocational school, technical school, or community college is not a requirement for becoming a plumber. Some plumbers leave high school and immediately start working.

Beginning plumbers do an apprenticeship and take classes at night or on weekends. You can find apprenticeship opportunities through the UA website. Some plumbing companies hire trainees and offer on-the-job training and educational assistance. The classroom component of a plumber's education can be done online, via distance learning. This allows you to get hands-on experience at a job and study at your own pace. Every person is different, so there is no one right way. A student's choice may depend on his or her personality, financial situation, or goals. There are benefits and drawbacks to each choice. When making the decision, students should carefully weigh their options.

An advantage of continuing to community college or technical school is that students can learn from experts. Teachers are available to answer questions. Students are also part of a community and can discuss what they're learning with their classmates. By working together, students at a community college can have a richer learning experience than they might have had trying to figure things out by themselves. Another advantage of school is that students can take classes in specialized topics relevant to plumbing. These classes give students a head start when they begin an apprenticeship program. Attending college give you the opportunity to take additional classes in art or business that might prove helpful later.

College or technical school costs money. Students will most likely not be able to work a full-time job while attending college and will have to work around their class schedule. However, many schools offer scholarships, grants, and other forms of financial aid that can help defray the cost of tuition. Classes at a community college or a local state university are less expensive than a four-year degree at a private school. Choosing a local college eliminates the cost of housing from the equation.

Community colleges offer other classes that can help in your career, such as business and communications, art, and foreign languages.

Some high school or vocational school graduates decide to begin an apprenticeship program. A UA apprenticeship lasts five years and incurs no student debt. Apprentices earn a competitive wage while they learn. Their schedule includes time in the classroom, workshop, and on the job. They learn math, science, how to read building plans, how to care for their tools, and safety.

A disadvantage of going to work right after high school is that everything will be focused on their job. They don't get the experience of interacting with other students and may miss out on other, non-plumbing classes they could take at a community college.

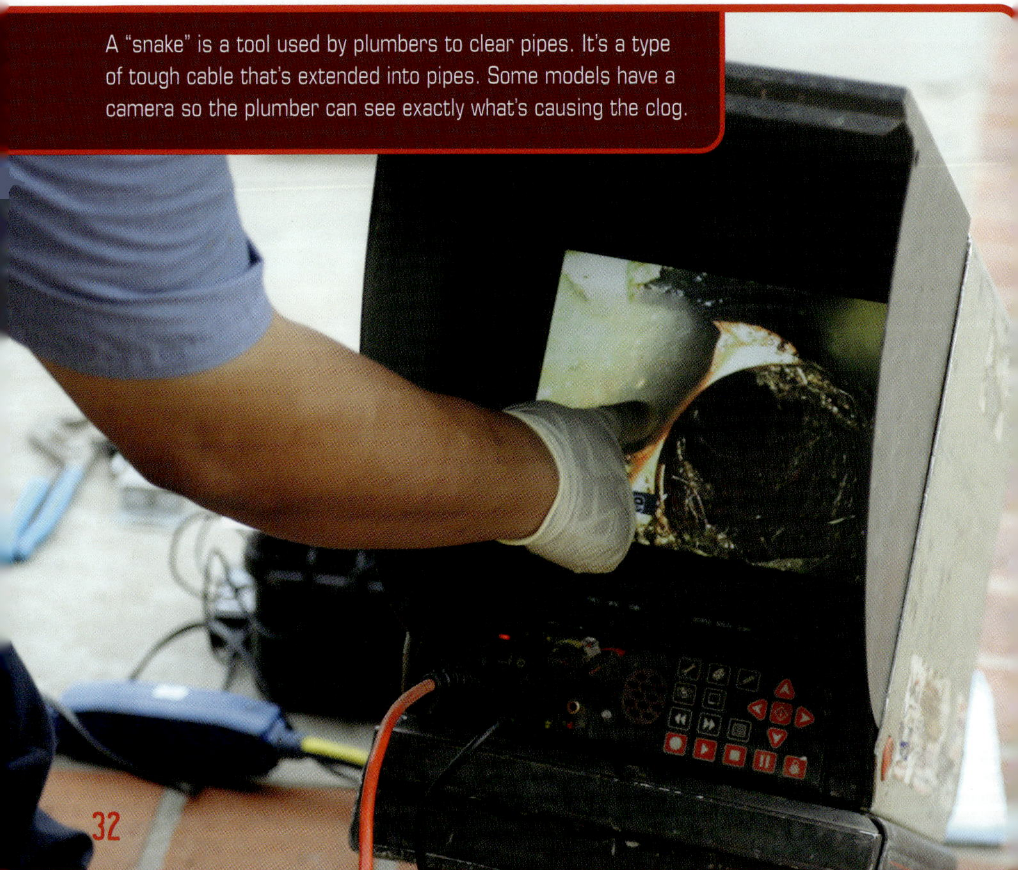

A "snake" is a tool used by plumbers to clear pipes. It's a type of tough cable that's extended into pipes. Some models have a camera so the plumber can see exactly what's causing the clog.

PLUMBING CODES

Building codes are laws passed by municipal governments. They are written to make sure that buildings are safe for the people who live and work in them. Some building codes are specific to plumbing. These rules and regulations are created so that people have safe drinking water and sanitary living conditions. The first such law was the English Public Health Code of 1848.

The codes are particularly concerned with keeping fresh water and wastewater separate, so people don't get sick. They specify safety measures for any plumbing work done in a factory, home, hospital, office, or school. A large part of a plumber's education is learning and understanding all plumbing codes.

Students who want more help with the decision of whether to apply to school or begin working should speak with their school guidance counselor. A guidance counselor can not only provide students with valuable career advice but can also help them find information about community colleges, trade schools, and apprenticeship programs. The UA website has information on apprenticeships, including some tailored for parents of prospective apprentices.

JOINING JOB CORPS

The U.S. Department of Labor runs a program called Job Corps for at-risk teens and young adults. The Job Corps offers courses in several construction trades, including plumbing. The program also helps teens and young adults ages 16 to 24 earn their high school diploma or GED. The program includes housing, meals, health care, and a stipend. Once students have completed the program, Job Corps helps them create résumés and find employment. Most Job Corps programs are considered pre-apprenticeships. Job Corps is an excellent option for those who are having a difficult time affording college. This program is free to anyone who qualifies for it.

JOINING THE MILITARY

Any place there are people, there's plumbing, and plumbers to fix it. Military installations are no exception. Joining the military is another way to prepare for a career in plumbing or pipe fitting. Plumbers and pipe fitters are needed in every branch of the military. Enlistees receive training in plumbing and pipe fitting in return for their service. This training is very similar to the kind of training they would receive in class or in an apprenticeship outside of the military without incurring student debt. To qualify, you need to have a minimum score on certain sections of the Armed Services Vocational Aptitude Battery (ASVAB) and meet all other enlistment requirements.

The Army offers an enlisted career path as a plumber. The Navy offers a career path as a utilitiesman, which includes training in several plumbing-related fields such as heating and cooling

In addition to learning professional careers skills, military construction specialists—including those trained for plumbing trades—often respond to civilian emergencies.

systems, and pipe laying. Believe it or not, you can even train for a plumbing career in the Air Force. Water and fuel systems maintenance specialists are responsible for plumbing-related tasks, including fire suppression systems.

Military plumbers and pipe fitters install and maintain pipe systems in buildings, ships, and aircraft. The experience that people gain from plumbing and pipe fitting in the military can be a great help when they attempt to establish a civilian plumbing career. Military plumbing experience can reduce the number of hours they have to spend in the classroom, or as an apprentice, before becoming a licensed plumber. The UA has programs to help veterans transition to civilian careers.

THE THINGS PEOPLE FLUSH BUT SHOULDN'T!

Plumbing systems, especially in houses, are intended to carry water. Toilets are designed to carry human waste and toilet paper. It's important to control what gets flushed or goes down the drains. Hair can accumulate in drains, particularly in the shower or tub, causing clogs. Thick fluids such as grease should never be poured down drains as it can accumulate in pipes, eventually causing clogs, and solid objects should never be flushed down the toilet.

Foreign objects like these can damage plumbing, requiring professional repair or replacement. Besides the potential damage to household plumbing, anything that goes down a drain eventually rejoins the community water supply. Wastewater from homes flows into the sewer system. From there it goes to a water treatment plant. There the water flows through filters and has chemicals added to it to neutralize any contaminants. The process takes about six hours.

A water treatment facility uses a system of filters, chemicals, and friendly bacteria to purify wastewater and return it to the municipal water supply.

A clogged toilet isn't just messy and expensive—it's a health hazard.

CHAPTER FOUR

APPRENTICESHIP

Most people who want a career in plumbing—or in any other building trade—start out as an apprentice. Aspiring plumbers get hands-on experience during their apprenticeship. An apprenticeship consists of working alongside an experienced plumber, known as a master plumber. During this time, apprentices learn everything they will need to know to become a licensed plumber.

WHAT'S AN APPRENTICESHIP?

An apprenticeship is an on-the-job training program. In addition to working with experienced plumbers, apprentices also take classes at night or on weekends. Depending on the program, some apprentices work four days a week and attend classes one day a week. Most apprenticeship programs last four or five years. In a UA apprenticeship program, apprentices are expected to spend about 2,000 hours working and about 200 hours taking classes.

Apprenticeship programs vary from state to state and from program to program. In some municipalities, apprentices are required to be licensed or registered to work in the plumbing industry. Generally, apprentices aren't allowed to work without supervision from a master plumber. Apprentices are paid a competitive wage—less than a licensed plumber, but probably better than many other student jobs, plus they don't accumulate student debt during their apprenticeship. For example, in Western New York, an apprentice plumber can earn $17 to $19 per hour.

Apprentices learn the trade from the ground up by observing and assisting a master plumber. They learn to read blueprints and building plans so they will know where to place pipes. They become familiar with the varieties of pipes and other plumbing materials, study building codes and learn important safety procedures as well as how to use all the tools needed to get the job done.

This apprentice is learning about boilers. Many plumbing firms are billed as plumbing and heating specialists.

WHAT ARE THE REQUIREMENTS?

Apprentices must be at least 18 years old and in good physical condition. Plumbing involves climbing on ladders, squeezing under sinks, and carrying heavy or awkward items. They also need good manual dexterity. In most cases, apprentices must have graduated from high school or have a GED. Apprenticeship programs often require that apprentices have a driver's license, and many programs require that apprentices pass a drug test. A birth certificate, or another document that proves that applicants are 18 or older, as well as documentation proving that the applicant is a citizen or legal immigrant, is sometimes requested.

Apprenticeships are generally run by unions or contractor organizations. Here is a list of organizations that sponsor plumbing apprenticeships:

- American Fire Sprinkler Association
- Associated Builders and Contractors
- Home Builders Institute of the National Association of Home Builders
- Mechanical Contractors Association of America
- Plumbing-Heating-Cooling Contractors Association
- National Fire Sprinkler Association
- United Association of Journeymen and Apprentices of the Plumbing and Pipe Fitting Industry of the United States and Canada
- Roto-Rooter

To find a local apprenticeship, students can check with one of these organizations or with their state's Department of Labor.

REQUIRED READING

In addition to the on-the-job training, apprentices spend time in the classroom. They study math, science, safety, first aid, many types of plumber's tools, various pipe systems, and many other topics. They also learn how to read blueprints and plans. There are many different programs available. Requirements vary from state to state. Here are two curriculums for comparison.

Penn Foster, a longtime leader in distance learning located in Scranton, Pennsylvania, offers a career diploma in plumbing. The program takes five to nine months to complete. It consists of eight courses and 35.7 continuing education units (CEU). It costs about $1,100.

- Introduction to Construction and Building Trades
- Introduction to Plumbing and Pipe Fitting
- Fundamentals of Plumbing
- Modern Plumbing
- Math for Plumbers
- Finish Plumbing
- Reading Piping Prints
- International Plumbing Code

The State University of New York (SUNY) Erie offers a course called Foundations of Plumbing. It's 145 course hours and takes about 12 months to complete. It costs about $2,200.

- Plumbing History, Codes, and Principles
- Tools of the Plumbing Trade
- First Aid and Safety
- Basic Math for Plumbing
- Water Supply, Water Sources, Waste Disposal, and Sewage Disposal
- Mechanical Properties and Protection of Building Materials and Structure
- Piping Materials Used in Plumbing Work
- Joining Methods for Drain, Waste, and Vent (DWV) and Pressure Piping
- Squares, Square Roots, and Basic Geometry
- Plumbing Fixtures
- Faucets and Related Devices
- Valves
- Water Heaters
- Building Plans, Drawings, and Scale Rulers
- Sketching
- Communication and Skills Professionalism
- Pipe Joining Techniques
- Special Applications of Plastic Pipe and Fittings
- Introduction to Welding
- Soldering, Brazing, Cutting, and Gas Welding
- Piping Materials, Sources, and Distribution for Potable Water
- Water Pipe Sizing: Main-and-Branch and Individual Run Systems
- Water Heaters and Hot Water Distribution
- Cross-Connection Protection and Pipe Identification
- Sewers & Sewage Disposal Methods
- Drainage Fixture Units
- Building Drains
- Stacks
- Applied Plumbing Mathematics
- Applied Geometric Concepts
- Properties of Water and Air

- Venting Plumbing Drainage Systems
- Sump Pumps, Sewage Pumps, and Sewage Ejectors
- Plumbing Traps
- Fixture Supports
- Hoisting and Rigging
- Safety Concepts
- Rough-In Sheets, Single Line Drawings, and Isometric Drawings
- Venting Plumbing Drainage Systems
- Winning Customer Service
- Customers Revealed
- Customer Expectations
- Customer Service: Why Do It?
- The Decline (and Revival) of Customer Service
- Moving Forward with the Four P's
- Traits of Outstanding Customer Reps
- Measuring Customer Service
- Customer Service Communication
- Helping Upset Customers

As you can see, the SUNY class is much more detailed. You need to do some research before deciding on a program so you can choose the right balance between cost and content.

Reading building plans and blueprints is an essential skill for plumbers. They need to understand how their systems integrate with electrical, HVAC, and all the other components of a building.

HOW MUCH WILL I BE PAID?

An apprenticeship is a job, so apprentices are paid and receive some benefits. The median wage for licensed plumbers is about $60,000 per year. Apprentice plumbers usually make about half that. As apprentices gain more experience, their wages go up. The kind of benefits they receive, such as health insurance, depend on the union they belong to or their employer. Apprentices usually receive benefits such as health insurance, as well as pensions and retirement savings plans.

TIPS FOR SUCCEEDING IN AN APPRENTICESHIP

Into Plumbing & Heating, a plumbing advice and discussion website, offers these insights for apprentices:

Ask questions. It's an apprentice's job to learn and that's how you get answers.

Stay organized. This goes for managing your time between work and classroom, as well as keeping your toolbox neat.

Network. It's never too early to start building a network of contacts. Right now, it might be that person who's a whiz at algebra that can help you get through a class. Later, it might be someone with a specific skill set that you might collaborate with on a job.

Keep yourself safe. This includes the obvious—always wear correct PPE and read all instructions for any equipment you use. It also means arriving at work well rested and with a clear head. (Save the late nights for weekends and vacation!)

Have a good work ethic. Always participate (unless instructed otherwise). Help with the cleanup, fetching and carrying.

Plumbers need to practice safe lifting. This is important because it keeps them safe and because a client paid for that sink, and it could be damaged if they drop it.

THINGS THAT AREN'T IN THE TEXTBOOK

Apprentices learn more than just plumbing skills from the plumbers who train them. If they work in residential plumbing, apprentices will learn good communication skills and how to work well with customers. For instance, it's important to be respectful of a client's home—work as neatly as possible and clean up afterwards.

Apprentices working on a construction site will learn how to interact with electricians, carpenters, and other professionals. They'll learn how to read plans and blueprints and work with architects, designers, and clients.

Plumbers who own their own business might also teach apprentices how to run their own company someday. They can give an honest appraisal of all the tasks involved—such as payroll, ordering supplies, billing, and taxes. This can help you decide if that interests you, or if you'd rather concentrate on plumbing, rather than business.

NOTHING NEW UNDER THE SUN

The concept of formal apprenticeship dates back hundreds of years—at least as far as the trade guilds of medieval Europe. Master craftsmen would accept apprentices for training, usually for a period of seven years. They would feed, clothe, and house the apprentices, in addition to teaching them their craft. At the end of their training, an apprentice would receive their own set of tools and become a journeyperson.

This system was brought to North America and practiced in the colonies. Eventually the system of apprenticeship died out as college education, rather than training with a master, became the accepted path to professional success in many fields. Some crafts, such as spinning and weaving, became automated. Business owners were able to hire unskilled factory workers instead of master craftsmen. However, the building trades have always required hands-on training.

In 1936, the UA's apprenticeship program became the first of its kind to be recognized by the U.S. Department of Labor. Today's five-year program includes 2,000 hours of on-the-job training and 216 hours of classroom instruction. Apprentices are paid while they train and complete the program with no student debt.

This whimsical statue is a monument to plumbers. It's located in Subotica, Serbia

CHAPTER FIVE

WHAT DO PLUMBERS DO ALL DAY?

The two main tasks of plumbers are installation and repair. Plumbers install new pipes and pipe systems. On residential jobs, plumbers may install plumbing and appliances such as dishwashers, washing machines, or hot water heaters. They install solar hot water systems and outdoor hot tubs.

When plumbers work on commercial jobs, they may also install specialized equipment such as a special pipe system in a laboratory that uses hazardous chemicals. They install sprinkler systems and water-cooled air-conditioning systems.

The other main task plumbers perform is repair. They find and fix leaks in pipes, faucets, and water lines. They unclog pipes and drains. During the winter, plumbers may be called to repair damaged pipes. Cold temperatures can cause the water inside pipes to freeze, and therefore expand, busting the pipe. Over time, residue can build up inside pipes and they need to be cleared out with a tool called a snake. Some types of pipes can crack as they get older, causing serious leaks. Sometimes tree roots can grow through underground pipes, rupturing them.

Occasionally, plumbers are called upon to "rescue" things that have accidentally gone down a drain, such as expensive rings or other jewelry. In these cases, plumbers use a cable with a small camera attached to locate the object. When the plumber finds the item, he or she can sometimes grab it with small pincers and pull it out. Other times, the fixture must be taken off the floor or wall to locate the missing object.

Snakes come in different sizes. This is a small, manual one used for narrow pipes.

This is a heavier, motorized snake being used to clear a sewer pipe.

INSTALLING PLUMBING IN A NEW HOUSE

Building a house takes many kinds of professionals. A pipelayer will be responsible for preparing the ground and laying the large pipes that will eventually connect the house to the main sewer and water lines. Carpenters called framers will assemble the skeleton of the house. They'll be followed by plumbers, electricians, and HVAC technicians.

All these people, including the plumber, will work closely with the blueprints and building plans from the architect and contractor. All the utilities a building needs must be installed so they don't conflict with one another. The plans tell the plumber where the fixtures will go. The plumber makes note of where the water line will come in from the street. They'll also note where the sewage line, which connects the house to the municipal sewage system or a septic tank, will go.

Based on the plans, the plumber will begin to lay out where the pipes will need to be placed. Once the pipes are roughly laid out, the plumber marks on the walls, ceilings, or floors where the pipes will go. They note obstacles the pipes will need to go around, such as lines for electricity. The plumber then takes careful measurements so they will have pipes of the correct length. The plumber must also make sure that installing pipes will not cause any other problems with the building. For instance, if the pipes are too heavy, they could pull away from their support and damage a wall or ceiling. Some appliances, such as washing machines, bathtubs, or showers, need several pipes. These fixtures need separate pipes for hot and cold water and a pipe to drain away wastewater.

In places where the temperature drops below freezing, they need to install shut-off valves for any outside water connections, so they can be turned off for the winter. The plumber will also need to make sure that all the plumbing in the house conforms to local building codes.

When a house is being built, plumbers collaborate with carpenters, electricians, and architects to be sure all the elements of the building work harmoniously.

When all marking and measuring is complete, the plumber begins cutting holes in walls, floors, or ceilings. Just like carpenters, plumbers live by the axiom "measure twice, cut once." The holes will allow the pipes to be attached to fixtures. After holes have been cut for every pipe, the plumber begins putting the pipes in place. Sometimes pipes must be hung using metal supports, and other times they are laid underground.

With the straight pipes in place, the plumber begins hooking them together with connectors. Connectors can be U-shaped, or they can be bent at an angle. This type of connector can connect a horizontal pipe to a vertical pipe. If a plumber is using metal pipes, sometimes he or she can bend them into the correct angle. Once the pipes are correctly connected, the plumber can begin to securely attach the pipes to each other. They attach pipes using different methods. PVC pipes can be glued, and metal pipes can be soldered together.

The next step is to attach the fixtures to the pipes. How the fixtures are attached depends on the fixture and the type of pipe being used. When all the pipes are attached to fixtures, the plumber begins testing all parts of the system. They turn all faucets on and off to make sure water is flowing and draining correctly. The plumber also checks the water pressure to make sure water is getting through pipes at the correct rate. If water is flowing too slowly or too quickly, the plumber must make adjustments.

Finally, a plumber must also set up a system of traps and vents. Traps are attached to the pipe that drains water away from a fixture, such as a sink. The trap holds a little of the water inside, which prevents gas from the sewer from coming up into the house or building. Vents go outside the building—usually through a roof—to allow air into the plumbing system. The air helps keep water flowing correctly. After all the pipes and ducts are in place, workers add insulation and drywall.

A new residential construction job can last from several days to a week or more. The length of the job depends on the size of the house, how many fixtures must be installed, and how many bathrooms are in the house. The time needed can increase if the plumber discovers any problems in the construction, or if they run into difficulties with municipal water, gas, or sewer pipes. A municipal building inspector must sign off on the project before people can move in.

A building inspector is a municipal employee. Their job is to make sure that buildings comply with local building codes. After they perform the final walk-through of a new building, they issue a Certificate of Occupancy. This means the building is safe for people to move in.

WHAT'S IN YOUR TOOLBOX?

A plumber will use all sorts of tools in their career. The types of tools used vary depending on the project, but most plumbers will have a fairly complete tool kit. This includes hand tools and power tools.

Plumbers often need to transport tools, pipes, and other supplies to the job site, so most of them own a truck or a van. It's important that a truck used for business is neat and clean, without any questionable bumper stickers. Magnetic car signs with your business information are easy to design. Beat up, unmarked vehicles loitering in a neighborhood make other residents nervous, but a respectable-looking van with your business information on the door can act as a good business card.

MEASURING TOOLS

Plumbers spend a lot of time measuring things. They measure where pipes will go. Then they measure the pipes. They must be very accurate. If they cut pipes wrong, those pieces of pipe might be wasted. If they don't connect correctly, there can be a terrible, leaky mess.

Plumbers sometimes use a regular tape measure. For jobs that must be extremely accurate, they use something called a steel rule (a rigid and more accurate ruler). They might also use a square (a ruler that resembles the letter L) for measuring right angles. Calipers or a micrometer make very precise, small measurements. Plumbers often mark their measurements with an ordinary pencil or pen, although they might also use a permanent marker to make darker lines that won't wear off. To make markings on sheet metal or metal pipes, plumbers can use a tool called a scriber. Plumbers use a tool called a center punch to mark the exact center of a circle where a hole will be drilled.

TOOLS OF THE TRADE

As a plumber, you'll rely on the contents of your toolbox. You need to invest in good quality professional tools or else you'll be replacing them more often than you'd like. You might consider a part-time job in a hardware store when you're old enough. Working in a big box store you'll see (and be able to handle) many different brands and variations of the same tool. However, if you work in a local hardware store, you won't see the same breadth of merchandise, but the owner probably knows a great deal about what he carries. Into Plumbing & Heating recommends the following tools for a new plumber:

- pipe cutters
- pipe wrenches
- pliers
- adjustable wrench
- tape measure
- utility knife
- torpedo level
- multi-bit screwdriver
- hammer
- permanent markers
- relevant PPE

Your instructor may have other suggestions or recommendations. As you become familiar with what's available, you'll discover your favorite brands.

DEMOLITION AND CUTTING TOOLS

Some repairs and renovations require opening up walls or floors to access pipes. Plumbers need to be able to cut through drywall and other materials. If they're trying to preserve the wall, they'll use a small, sharp tool called a keyhole saw to cause minimal damage. If they need to remove old or damaged floors or walls, they might use a pry bar.

Once they access the pipes, they might need to remove old or damaged sections, so they need tools that will cut metal. Plumbers often use tubing cutters to cut pipes, although some kinds of pipe require special tools to cut. Copper pipe is generally cut with hacksaws, and chain-link cutters can be used to cut wide cast-iron pipe. The links on chain-link cutters look like a bicycle chain. They can be wrapped around pipes of various sizes. The links are then tightened to cut through the pipe.

Plumbers carry wire cutters, as well as a few different types of files. They use files to smooth the rough edges left after they cut metal. Tin snips are useful for cutting sheet metal. Some types of tin snips can cut curves, while others are better at cutting straight lines.

A sturdy toolbox or caddy is a wise investment for an aspiring plumber.

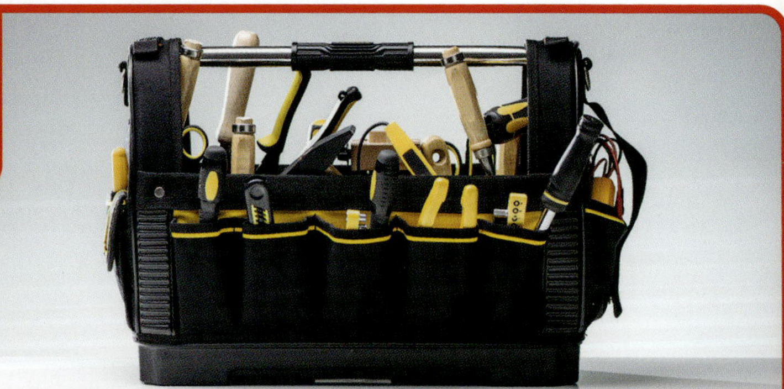

WRENCHES

Wrenches and ratchets are the most-used tools in a plumber's toolbox. They always have a wide assortment with them on a job. Wrenches are used to loosen or tighten fasteners, and they also help plumbers get a good grip on a pipe. There are many types of wrenches, including adjustable, basin, pipe, socket, and strap wrenches. Plumbers usually have many wrenches in a variety of sizes. Some are designed to grip large bolts or heavy pipes, and others are small and made to fit into narrow spaces.

Over the course of their career, a plumber will accumulate many types and sizes of wrenches.

SOLDERING IRONS AND TORCHES

Pipes need to be connected securely so they don't leak. Plumbers use special tools to mend and connect metal pipes. One of these is a soldering iron. Solder is a mixture of metals that melt at a lower temperature than the pipe the plumber wants to connect. Solder comes in wire form or as a bar.

A soldering iron works by heating the solder until it melts. Then the plumber applies the melted solder to both halves of a pipe. When the solder cools, it also hardens, and the pipes are securely connected. When connecting thicker pipes, plumbers use a different tool to melt the solder. This is called a heat torch, which is powered by propane and other types of gases. A heat torch can create much higher temperatures, which are better for melting solder.

Plumbers are trained to use soldering irons or heat torches. They need to know how to use these tools safely, so they don't hurt themselves or set off fire alarms. When using a torch powered by any kind of gas, they need to be sure their workspace has adequate ventilation.

PLUNGERS AND AUGERS

One of the most common tools a plumber uses is a plunger. You probably have at least one in your home. Plungers clear blockages by sucking air and water out of the drain and then forcing it back in. There are two different designs—one for toilets and one for sinks.

Another tool plumbers use to clear blocked pipes in an auger. Augers are flexible tubes with special attachments on the end. A plumber feeds an auger into a blocked pipe. When it reaches the blockage, the plumber twists the attachments to loosen the blockage. Sometimes plumbers attach augers to an electric drill. The drill helps rotate the attachments to exert more force on the blockage.

GENERAL AND SAFETY TOOLS

In addition to their collection of wrenches, plumbers carry a variety of other tools. These include screwdrivers, pliers, and hammers. A sturdy, reliable flashlight is a must. A headlamp (a bright flashlight worn on an elastic band around the head) is another good option. Plumbers also use mirrors to see around corners when working on a job where space is limited.

Plumbers use flashlights and headlamps to inspect dark nooks and crannies behind walls and under sinks.

On the job, plumbers generally just wear jeans or other long, sturdy pants and a T-shirt. Since plumbing can be a dirty job, some plumbers wear coveralls to keep their regular clothing clean. A coverall also looks more professional. A neat appearance is important for residential plumbers who work in clients' homes.

A plumber's tool kit should also contain appropriate PPE. Plumbers protect their hands with gloves when working with sharp metal or hot materials. They should have a few different kinds for use in different circumstances. They need eye protection when using cutting tools. When plumbers use welding equipment, they use protective gear, especially a face shield and heavy gloves. To protect their feet from falling pipes or tools, they generally wear steel-toed boots. Large construction sites often require all workers, including plumbers, to wear hard hats for their protection.

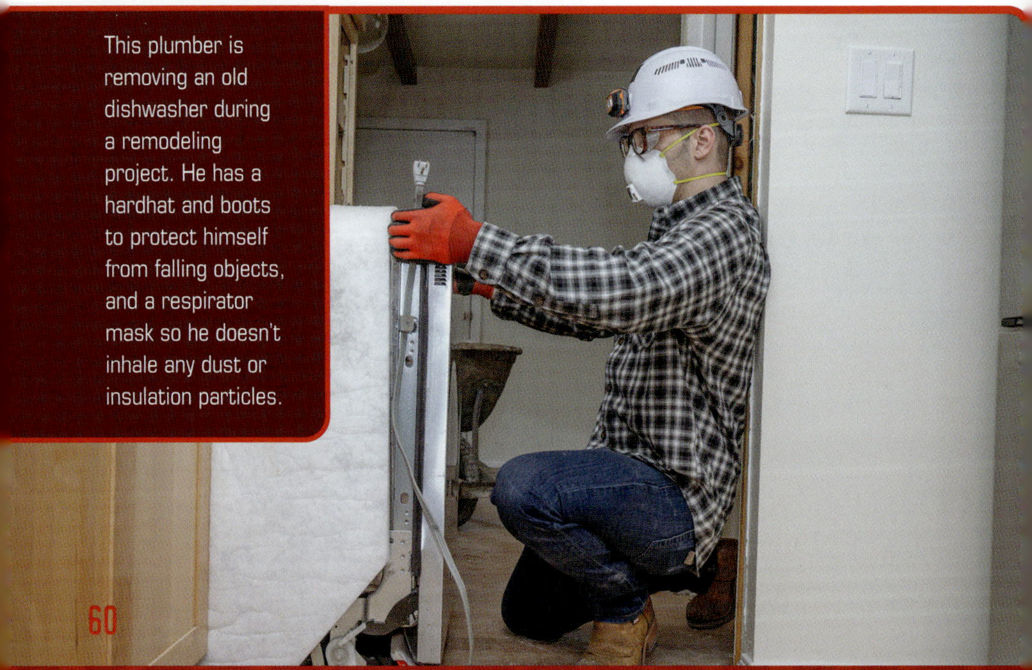

This plumber is removing an old dishwasher during a remodeling project. He has a hardhat and boots to protect himself from falling objects, and a respirator mask so he doesn't inhale any dust or insulation particles.

Plumbers should carry cleaning materials. Some residential plumbing companies equip their plumbers with shoe covers and paper mats to put down in clients' homes. Cleaning up after the job shows respect for their client's property and leaves a favorable impression—very important in this day of instant online reviews.

ALL KINDS OF PIPES

Plumbers generally choose pipes made of copper or plastic for installation in a house. Residential projects usually don't require a lot of water to flow through pipes, so smaller pipes are generally used for these projects. One or two plumbers or plumber's helpers can install these kinds of pipes.

Plastic pipes are commonly used in residences. There are several types of plastic pipe, including polyvinyl chloride (PVC), cross-linked polyethylene (PEX), and Acrylonitrile butadiene styrene (ABS). PVC can carry only cold water. PVC pipes meet current safety standards, however there are concerns they may leach harmful chemicals into drinking water. PEX pipes can carry hot or cold water, however, they deteriorate in sunlight and can be used only indoors. Some studies show they may leach chemicals into drinking water, so California plumbing codes ban their use. ABS is a type of plastic pipe used for drains and wastewater. It's resistant to cold, but warps in heat.

Copper pipe is also used in homes. It can carry hot or cold water. It's more expensive than plastic but can last for up to 50 years. Copper resists corrosion and can be recycled.

Although PVC is much more common today, plumbers still need the tools and know-how to handle galvanized steel pipes and fittings like those pictured.

In some older homes, galvanized steel was used. If plumbers make repairs to older homes, they must know how to work with galvanized pipe. Today, many plumbers will simply update plumbing systems by replacing galvanized pipe with newer types of pipes. They may even encounter cast iron pipes in older homes or water systems.

Plumbers also use small tubes for some small jobs. For example, tubing is used to connect an automatic ice maker in a refrigerator to a water supply.

SAFETY AND FIRST AID

As in any construction trade, safety is a major concern for plumbers. They work with sharp tools and tools that generate heat. It's important for them to understand how to handle those tools safely and use the proper PPE.

They need to understand how chemicals affect people and how they react if mixed. Store-bought drain cleaning fluid contains caustic ingredients. If a client has already applied some to a clog, the plumber needs to know so they can protect themselves. They also need to be sure the drain cleaner is completely rinsed away before using cleaning materials such as bleach. Plumbers in industrial settings might work with pipes that contain steam or chemicals.

Plumbers on construction sites lift heavy objects, climb ladders, and work in buildings that might not have walls. They need to practice safe lifting techniques and always be aware of their surroundings. Since construction is hard manual labor that generally takes place in the summer, they must be aware of their exposure to sun and heat.

For all these reasons, it's a good idea for a plumber to take the Occupational Safety and Health Administration (OSHA) 10-hour safety program, even if it's not a strict requirement for their location or type of employment. A first aid class can also be beneficial.

Sewers and municipal water supply systems service many homes and businesses. They need to carry much more water than a single house uses. These systems require much larger pipes. Often, they're made from cast iron. To install large pipes such as these, plumbers need to work with a team. The team might include experienced pipelayers and pipe fitters. Together, they use construction machinery such as backhoes to dig trenches for the pipes and cranes to move them. This is specialized work that requires extensive training.

CONNECTING ALL THOSE PIPES

To carry water or other materials, pipes need to be connected. Different materials are used to connect different types of pipes. A plumber can use screws or bolts to connect metal pipes. Metal pipes can also be soldered together. Plastic pipes can be joined by special glue. (For PVC pipes, this involves treating the pipe with solvent before applying the glue.) PEX pipes are connected by a method called crimping.

Plumbers join pipes with small devices called fittings. One type of fitting is called a coupling. A coupling is a short length of pipe, usually of the same material as the pipes being attached. Couplings can attach pipes of the same size or pipes that are two different sizes. There are fittings that can be used to connect PEX pipe to PVC or copper pipes.

Other fittings connect more than two pipes. Tees attach three pipes together. They are called tees because they look like the letter "T." They connect two pipes in a straight line and a third pipe perpendicular to the other two. Plumbers use a fitting called a cross to connect four pipes.

Plumbers can use fittings to create a bend in a pipe. These fittings are called elbows, or "ells." Like couplings, they can connect pipes of the same size or of two different sizes. Fittings such as caps and plugs can be put on one end of a pipe to seal it off.

Just like pipes, connectors come in many different shapes and sizes.

CHAPTER SIX

GETTING YOUR LICENSE

Getting a license is a huge milestone for a plumber. In most places, it's illegal to perform unsupervised plumbing work without a license. Some licenses are issued by state governments. Other are issued on a local level. For example, New York licenses plumbers at the local, rather than state level. Licensing requirements for New York City are particularly strict.

Generally, a plumber who's obtained their degree or completed an apprenticeship can apply to take a licensing exam. Depending on the location where they're applying for a license, they may have to fulfill other requirements, such as passing a drug test or a criminal background check. It's important to understand the requirements for the location where you plan to work and if that license is recognized in any other municipality.

Licensing exams vary from one place to another. To get a license, a plumber must pass a test on a variety of plumbing skills, as well as the local plumbing codes. This might include both a written and a practical exam, with a required minimum score.

Generally, there are two different tests: one for a journeyperson and one for a master plumber. Journeyperson licenses are for people who have finished their apprenticeships and have worked as a plumber for a certain number of years. Master licenses are for plumbers who already have a journeyperson license and have also worked for a required number of hours and taken additional night or weekend classes.

There's no single licensing exam, so it's important to review whatever outline or syllabus your licensing agency provides. There are some general study guides available from test prep publishers.

In addition to licenses for journeypersons and master plumbers, some states issue licenses for apprentices. Others have an additional license called a residential license. This license is for plumbers who have finished an apprenticeship but have not worked for as many years as a journeyperson. Some states license plumbers as contractors, rather than journeypersons or masters.

It isn't possible for a plumber to get certified nationally. Instead, each state or local town has different licensing requirements and exams. Plumbers must be familiar with their state and local plumbing codes. If a plumber moves to a different state or city, they will most likely need a new license to work in the area.

Licensing exams are usually made up of multiple choice, true or false, and fill-in-the-blank questions. These tests have questions on topics such as:

- typical plumbing fixtures used in homes
- specialized fixtures, such as large dishwashers used in restaurants
- the procedure for connecting a building to a public sewage system
- types of pipes to use for particular jobs
- safety
- local plumbing codes
- local business law
- insurance

Some municipalities also require a practical exam. Licenses generally need to be renewed periodically, with proof of the required amount of continuing education.

Licensing exams can be difficult, and as mentioned, vary from place to place. Some may have a lot of business or local law material. However, the bulk of most exams are concerned with the basic principles of plumbing. Anyone who studies hard can eventually pass the test.

Licensing exams are usually given at professional testing centers, either on a computer or with paper and pencil. You generally need to bring at least one form of government-issued identification. Some places may allow you to bring specific references.

Libraries and bookstores carry test preparation books that can help plumbers pass the exam. Because the tests are all different, commercial test prep material will likely concentrate on general plumbing skills and knowledge. Colleges and trade schools offer test preparation classes that can also help. These classes are usually held on nights and weekends. However, taking a class isn't always necessary—plumbers can also study on their own for the exam. Public libraries sometimes have online practice tests or classes that plumbers can take. Some plumbers choose to study with another plumber who is also preparing to take the licensing exam or get help from plumbers who have already passed the exam.

ONE ON ONE WITH A PLUMBER

Here are some insights from a licensed plumber who held several other jobs until settling on a rewarding career in plumbing.

What do you like about plumbing?
I like to be able to work with my hands and to work on a project from start to finish. I also like being able to work independently. Plumbing is a good trade. There are good opportunities for working your way up. For example, you can become an estimator or project manager. You can also start your own business.

What was your career path?
I worked in a few different fields before becoming a

plumber. I worked in landscaping and did some concrete work. Then I began fixing and installing oil burners. When I was 30 years old, I began working as a plumber's apprentice and went to night school. I served three years of an apprenticeship and then took the licensing exam. (My state now requires a five-year apprenticeship, but at the time I did it, my apprenticeship was only three years long.)

What do you recommend students do if they want to be a plumber?
I would recommend going to vocational school. You should definitely study math. Geometry can help you a lot.

What should people do to prepare for the licensing exam?
You don't necessarily need to take an exam preparation class. Most people do OK studying on their own for the exam. However, you have to put time into studying if you want to pass.

Do you see good opportunities for people who want to be plumbers?
Yes, there is going to be a huge demand in the coming years. Many plumbers will be retiring soon. And, although the building boom is over, a lot of existing buildings are being retrofitted with green improvements.

GOING GREEN

Global warming, more correctly referred to as climate change, has been making headlines for some time. Consumers are becoming more eco-conscious in the things they buy and the way they live. This extends to the plumbing and heating systems in their homes.

Making environmentally friendly improvements in a building's plumbing can save homeowners or business owners money in water or energy costs. And, of course, it also helps the environment by preserving natural resources.

"Green plumbing" can play a big role in making buildings more energy efficient and environmentally friendly, and there are several eco-friendly changes that plumbers can make in homes and buildings. An example of a simple change is installing high-efficiency fixtures, such as low-flow or high-efficiency toilets. Other toilets compost waste, rather than using any water to flush. Some modern urinals actually use no water at all. There are also low-flow showers and tankless hot water heaters available. Front-loading washing machines use much less water than top-loading machines, and modern dishwashers use less water than older models. Although these items are a big-budget initial purchase, over time they pay for themselves in lowered water and electric charges.

For people who are even more serious about greening their building, plumbers can make more extensive changes as well. For instance, they might install radiant heating or solar heating systems, or they may design and install gray water systems. They might also replace wasteful lawn sprinkler systems with drip irrigation systems.

Plumbers can take courses in green plumbing to add to their set of skills. Trade and vocational schools are adding courses in green technology to their plumbing training programs. Some schools and companies also offer courses for certifying plumbers in green technologies, such as solar heating installation and repair.

Of course, the most eco-friendly thing people can do is get that leaky faucet fixed. Did you know that a dripping faucet can waste as much as 3,000 gallons of water a year? That's about 180 showers!

This is a hydronic radiant heating system. Hot water will be pumped through these tubes to heat the room. After installation, they'll be covered by the top layer of flooring.

HEATING THINGS UP

Two types of green heating systems rely on plumbing to operate. These are solar heating systems and hydronic radiant heating systems. Solar systems use solar energy to generate electricity and to warm water or create electricity. Solar power is a clean, renewable resource. This means that using it doesn't create pollution, and that it's not possible to use it up.

Hydronic radiant heat consists of small pipes or tubes that are concealed underneath flooring and carry hot water. This heat radiates upward from the floor. Many heating systems rely on forced air—that is, heated air blowing from a duct. A lot of heat is lost in the process of blowing from the furnace throughout the building. Also, since ducts are located inside walls, over time they accumulate dust, mold, and other allergens, which are then blown through the system and circulated along with the warm air. Since radiant heating is so efficient, it costs homeowners less money to heat their building. Sometimes radiant heating is installed in the walls or ceilings of a building as well.

GRAY WATER SYSTEMS

Gray water recycling systems are another popular green plumbing technology. Gray water is wastewater generated by dishwashers, washing machines, sinks, and showers. It does not include water that's been flushed in the toilet with waste. Sometimes gray water is filtered or processed. It can then be used as water to be flushed in toilets. Gray water can be stored and then reused to water outdoor plants. When gray water is used for gardening, it's a good idea to use biodegradable soap and detergent products. Plumbers can create and install gray water systems in homes and other buildings.

Women have a great deal to offer the plumbing industry. The UA is actively trying to recruit more women to the trade, and Home Depot has a scholarship fund especially for women who want to attend trade school for the construction industry.

A CAREER FOR WOMEN

As of 2023, the BLS reported that out of 610,000 plumbers, pipe fitters, and steamfitters in the United States, 1.1 percent were women. Out of 52,000 pipelayers, 2.4 percent are women. Traditionally, plumbing, like most construction trades, has been considered a male-only profession. Some people still believe women can't handle the heavy physical work that male plumbers do. But this attitude is slowly changing, and many women are realizing that plumbing is a worthwhile career that pays well.

Women plumbers ultimately find they can handle the physical challenges of the job just as well as men. Mostly, it involves looking at the job from all angles and finding a solution that doesn't rely on brute strength.

Believe it or not, the first female master plumber in the United States got her license in 1951. Lillian Ann Baumbach Jacobs (1930–2000) took the master plumber's exam at the age of 21, along with six men—four of whom failed. Currently, there are few role models for young female plumbers to look up to. One of them is Adrienne Bennett, who was the first African American woman to become a master plumber in 1987. She worked as a master plumber, project manager, plumbing inspector, and code enforcement officer before starting her own plumbing and water conservation company in 2008.

Women are totally capable of working in construction trades. In fact, women often think of better, safer ways to do things precisely because they don't rely on brute strength.

Young women may not realize there are opportunities in the plumbing profession. That may change as more women enter the profession. It can be helpful for young women who want to be plumbers to try and find a female plumber who works in their area. Experienced female plumbers may be willing to discuss the advantages of a career in plumbing or act as a mentor to a novice. Young women should also look for apprenticeship programs that specifically encourage women to apply, such as the Home Depot Foundation's Path to Pro Scholarship for Women.

Women have been a valuable part of the workforce for many decades now. However, the attitude of some male plumbers has not necessarily reflected that fact. In some cases, male plumbers have harassed their female colleagues. Some male customers don't think women were capable of doing the job. On the other hand, women clients, especially those who live alone, are more comfortable having a having a female plumber work in their home.

Many female plumbers say it's possible to get past those attitudes. Sometimes they even change sexist male plumber's minds by showing how well women can do the job. This is not the only way in which female plumbers can face gender discrimination in the workplace, however. Sometimes, qualified female plumbers might not get hired for a job simply because they aren't male. This is changing as cultural attitudes evolve. In addition, the need for competent plumbers is increasing as older workers retire. Some female plumbers avoid discrimination by starting their own business.

WHAT CAN YOU DO WITH THAT LICENSE?

Once plumbers are licensed, they have several career options. They can earn a very comfortable living carrying out residential repairs, installations, and renovations, or in construction. Licensed plumbers can also train and supervise other plumbers. A licensed master plumber can train an apprentice or journeyperson plumber.

Licensed master plumbers can also become plumbing inspectors. Plumbing inspectors approve plans for plumbing work and issue permits if needed. They check the work of other plumbers to make sure it meets local plumbing codes and issue citations for violations.

There will always be work for licensed residential plumbers, especially repair work.

Licensed plumbers can become plumbing estimators. Estimators figure out how much time a project will take, what materials are needed, and how much the job will cost. They often work for companies that build large buildings or groups of buildings, such as apartment complexes. Estimators work with engineers and architects before a building project begins. They need strong computer and communications skills and familiarity with local building codes.

Plumbers that start their own business generally begin by working on their own or with a business partner. As their business builds, they can hire other people to work for them, such as an office manager. In some cases, they might hire additional plumbers to help with the workload or other workers that can offer additional services. For instance, a business owner might hire a person to work on heating or air-conditioning systems or someone who can build or clean septic systems.

Plumbers can also apply their knowledge and expertise to other business pursuits. They might try their hand at starting their own plumbing supply company or contracting firm. They might even team up with a landscape designer to start a company that installs irrigation systems. These types of watering systems might be used on farms to grow crops. Other types of irrigation systems might be set up on residential or business lawns or gardens.

WHAT DOES THE FUTURE HOLD?

Regardless of the state of the economy, there will always be opportunities for plumbers. Plumbers are valued professionals in any community. They keep the water flowing in our kitchens, bathrooms, and laundry rooms. Without them we'd have no showers, clean clothes, or fresh drinking water. And let's not even consider what happens when the toilet won't flush!

Any building people spend time in has a plumbing system and at some point, some part of that system will require a plumber's attention. Running water and a functioning sanitary system are essential. No matter what else must be put on hold, people will usually find a way to pay for repairs to their plumbing.

If you're not afraid of hard work, and you enjoy the challenge of making a complex system work, a career as a plumber might be right for you.

Plumbing is far from an old-fashioned job. Today's plumbers work with cutting-edge technology such as solar water heating systems.

10 GREAT QUESTIONS TO ASK A LICENSED PLUMBER

Here are some questions you can ask a licensed plumber.

1. Did you get a degree or complete an apprenticeship?
2. Are you a journeyperson or a master plumber?
3. Are there any high school classes or activities you recommend?
4. What's your favorite part of your job?
5. Do you like working on your own or as part of a team?
6. Are there any books you recommend I read? Industry blogs or magazines that are worth following?
7. How has "green plumbing" affected your career?
8. Do you go to conventions or trade shows to learn about new plumbing industry innovations?
9. Do you belong to a union or other professional organization?
10. Is there anything you wish someone had told you when you were considering this career?

What other questions can you think of?

Becoming a licensed plumber is a solid career choice. It will ensure you a well-paying job as a valued member of any community.

GLOSSARY

blueprint: A detailed building plan created by an architect.

citizen: A legal resident of a country.

colleague: An associate who works in the same profession.

compost: To break down organic matter in order to reuse it as a fertilizer.

contractor: A person hired to get a particular job done.

coverall: A one-piece outfit worn over regular clothes.

defray: To provide for the payment of something.

demolition: The act of tearing down an existing structure.

fire retardant: A substance that is used to put out or slow down a fire.

gender discrimination: Treating people unfairly based on whether they are male or female.

legal immigrant: Someone who has permission to live and work in a foreign country.

mechanism: A piece of machinery.

municipal: Something that is owned or operated by a city or town government.

obstacle: Something that stands in the way of a goal or objective.

pension: A salary paid to a worker after retirement.

perpendicular: Forming a right angle with something else.

propane: A gas that can be used as fuel.

remodel: To change or improve a structure.

residential plumber: A plumber who works on projects in private homes.

retrofit: To install new parts or equipment in something that is older. For instance, a plumber might retrofit a home by replacing old fixtures with newer, more efficient ones.

scaffolding: A temporary platform, or system of platforms, used to hold workers on a job site.

septic tank: A tank in which sewage is broken down by bacteria.

sewage: Waste material carried away by pipes.

FOR MORE INFORMATION

ASSOCIATED BUILDERS AND CONTRACTORS

440 1st Street, NW, Suite 200
Washington, D.C. 20001
(202) 595-1505
Website: abc.org
Facebook: @ABCNational
Instagram: @abc_national
ABC is a national construction industry trade association founded in 1950.

CANADA GREEN BUILDING COUNCIL

100 Murray Street, Suite 400
Ottawa, ON K1N 0A1
Canada
(866) 941-1184
Website: cagbc.org
Facebook and Instagram: @cagbc
The CAGBC is an organization that supports green building and retrofitting efforts in the Canadian real estate and construction industries.

GREEN PLUMBERS USA

928 2nd Street
Sacramento, CA 95814
(916) 642-5174
Website: greenplumbersamerica.com
Facebook: @greenplumbersusa
Green Plumbers USA trains plumbers in water conservation and eco-friendly plumbing techniques.

HOME BUILDERS INSTITUTE

1201 15th Street NW, Sixth Floor
Washington, D.C. 20005
(202) 371-0600
Website: hbi.org
Facebook and Instagram: @HBIBuildingcareers
The HBI provides free pre-apprenticeship training in a variety of trades.

JOB CORPS

200 Constitution Avenue NW, Room N4459
Washington, D.C. 20210
(800) 733-JOBS [5627]
Website: jobcorps.gov
Facebook and Instagram: @DOLJobCorps
The Job Corps is a Department of Labor program that provides free job training for young people.

MECHANICAL CONTRACTORS ASSOCIATION OF CANADA

280 Albert Street
Ottawa, ON K1P 5G8
Canada
(613) 232 0492
Website: mcac.ca
MCAC is a professional organization for Canadians who work in construction-related industries.

NATIONAL ASSOCIATION OF WOMEN IN CONSTRUCTION (NAWIC)

327 S. Adams Street
Fort Worth, TX 76104
(800) 552-3506
Website: nawic.org
Facebook and Instagram: @nawicnational
The NAWIC was offers education and networking opportunities to women in the construction industry.

NATIONAL CENTER FOR CONSTRUCTION EDUCATION AND RESEARCH

13614 Progress Blvd.
Alachua, FL 32615
(888) 622-3720
Website: nccer.org
Facebook and Instagram: @NCCER
The NCCER is a nonprofit foundation founded in 1996. They offer technical education and training for construction industry professionals.

PLUMBING-HEATING-COOLING CONTRACTORS ASSOCIATION

180 S. Washington Street, Suite 100
Falls Church, VA 22046
(800) 533-7694
Website: phccweb.org
Facebook: @PHCCNational
Instagram: @naphcc
Since 1883, PHCC has been a leading professional organization for plumbing and HVAC workers.

UNITED ASSOCIATION OF JOURNEYMEN AND APPRENTICES IN THE PLUMBING AND PIPE FITTING INDUSTRY OF THE UNITED STATES AND CANADA (UA)

United Association Building
3 Park Place
Annapolis, MD 21401
(410) 269-2000
Website: ua.org
Facebook: @UnitedAssociation
Instagram: @united associationhq
The UA is the union that represents most plumbing professionals in the United States and Canada.

U.S GREEN BUILDING COUNCIL

2101 L Street NW, Suite 600
Washington, D.C. 20037
(202) 848-7422
Website: usgbc.org
Facebook and Instagram: @usgbc
The USGBC is an organization that promoted green building practices.

FOR FURTHER READING

Bennett, Penelope M. *A Beginner's Guide to Understanding and Mastering Plumbing Basics: Unlock the Secrets of Plumbing with Easy-to-Follow Instructions and Expert Tips.* Independently Published, 2023.

Blankenbaker, E. Keith. *Modern Plumbing*. Tinley Park, IL: The Goodheart-Wilcox Company, Inc., 2022.

Carosso, Juan. *At Your Best as a Plumber: Your Playbook for Building a Successful Career and Launching a Thriving Small Business as a Plumber*. New York: Skyhorse Publishing, 2018.

Given-Wilson, Rachel and Simone Payment. *Your Future as a Plumber*. New York, NY: The Rosen Publishing Group, Inc., 2020.

Hemp, Peter. *Plumbing a House*. Independently Published, 2020.

Kamberg, Mary-Lane. *A Career As a Plumber, Pipefitter, or Steamfitter*. New York, NY: Rosen YA, 2019.

Kibert, Charles J. *Sustainable Construction: Green Building Design and Delivery*. Hoboken, NJ: Wiley, 2022.

Santore, Marcia. *Plumbers: A Practical Career Guide*. Lanham, MD: Rowman & Littlefield, 2020.

INDEX

M

N

O

P

R

ABOUT THE AUTHOR

KATHLEEN A. KLATTE is the author of many nonfiction books for children and teens. Topics range from animals and nature to constitutional law to unusual career choices. She lives in New York with one cat and far too many books and Legos.

PHOTO CREDITS

Photo credits:Cover, p. 1 Kostiantyn Voitenko/Shutterstock.com; pp. 1-96 Merydolla/Shutterstock.com; pp. 4, 79 Pixel-Shot/Shutterstock.com; p. 5 Kwangmoozaa/Shutterstock.com; p. 7 Klara Avsenik Zagar/Shutterstock.com; p. 8 mountainpix/Shutterstock.com; p. 9 Felix Mizioznikov/Shutterstock.com; pp. 11, 53, 56 , 81 Andrey_Popov/Shutterstock.com; p. 13 Scott Heaney/Shutterstock.com; p. 14 Paul Tessier/Shutterstock.com; p. 17 Glynnis Jones/Shutterstock.com; p. 19 zedspider/Shutterstock.com; p. 21 B Brown/Shutterstock.com; p. 23 AY Amazefoto/Shutterstock.com; p. 25 ZUMA Press, Inc. / Alamy Stock Photo; p. 27 Drazen Zigic/Shutterstock.com; p. 29 goodluz/Shutterstock.com; p. 31 Jacob Lund/Shutterstock.com; p. 32 mikeledray/Shutterstock.com; p. 35 SviatlanaLaza/Shutterstock.com; p. 36 PBabic/Shutterstock.com; p. 37 Andrey_Kuzmin/Shutterstock.com; p. 39 Daisy Daisy/Shutterstock.com; p. 43 theshots.co/Shutterstock.com; p. 45 MrcTeam/Shutterstock.com; p. 47 Zarko Prusac/Shutterstock.com; p. 49 Victor Moussa/Shutterstock.com; p. 49 pusit nimnakorn/Shutterstock.com; p. 51 Vanessa Belfiore/Shuttestock.com; p. 57 Andrii Medvediuk/Shutterstock.com; p. 59 Nor Gal/Shutterstock.com; p. 60 David Spates/Shutterstock.com; p. 62 linerpics/Shutterstock.com; p. 65 mihalec/Shutterstock.com; p. 67 Elnur/Shutterstock.com; p. 69 SuPatMaN/Shutterstock.com; p. 73 dotshock/Shutterstock.com; p. 75 Juice Dash/Shutterstock.com; p. 77 Maridav/Shutterstock.com; p. 83 SpeedKingz/Shutterstock.com.